*LOVE AS IT IS*

*LOVE AS IT IS*
*by Marilyn Bowering*

*For Brian,*
*with best wishes,*
*Marilyn Bowering.*

A Porcépic Book
Beach Holme Publishers Ltd.
Victoria, B.C.

This edition is published by Beach Holme Publishers Ltd,
4252 Commerce Circle, Victoria, B.C. V8Z 4M2.
This is a Porcépic Book.

Editor: David Godfrey
Production Editor: Elspeth Haughton
Cover Designer: Christine Toller
Cover Image: Mercedes Carbonell


*Canadian Cataloguing in Publication Data*

Bowering, Marilyn, 1949-
  Love as it is

  Poems.
  ISBN 0-88878-330-2

  1. Sand, George, 1804-1876—Poetry. 2. Chopin,Frédéric, 1810-1849
—Poetry. I. Title.
PS8553.093L6 1993        C811'.54        C93-091098-2
PR9199.3.B69L6 1993

*for Stan, who sat me down with
Chopin's letters,
and in memory of Margaret Wilson*

# CONTENTS

*Love above all, don't you agree?*
*Love above all when one's star*
*is in the ascendent, art above all*
*when the star is in decline.*
*Listen to the voice that sings love*
*and not to the voice that explains it.*

George Sand
(*Aurore Dudevant*)

ANTIQUITIES

## I Have Been Dreaming About the Wife

I have been dreaming about the wife
of a newly dead man. I have heard the air

thicken with news, and voices saying to her,
*Christine, you are wearing a red sweater.*

That the dead notice such things,
or that we think the dead miss us so

they are compelled to say,
*Do not wonder where I am,*

*I am here, with you!*

I have seen a man touch a woman
only so that he, himself, will not disappear.

I have watched the wife of the newly dead man
buy a waterfall of colour to wear.

*Christine, I like the pink stockings,*
*Christine, I like the way you wear your hair.*

*No, don't change anything,*
*stay how you were.*

In the dream no one is beautiful,
the dead man does not appear,

only his wife, and the voices saying:
*Christine, you are familiar.*

## Being True

I am in prison.
Now you cannot find me.
I make a prison in the dark with my body.
I make this prison so I will not escape you.

Dance with me. On this small concrete floor,
let your bare feet feel the cold.
The keys are here,
under my pillow.

Dance out of the dark and away.

Unlock these handcuffs
so that I may touch you.
What happens when the four walls break?

Visiting hour. We have nothing to say.
Let us use our lips to kiss.
I know how to love.  It will come back.

I want you to go.
I want you to find me in this dark
and pull me out.

Let us meet somewhere else.

If I do not dream,
if I have no dreams to betray me.

### The Red Factory
#### for Herbert Dacker

Near where I lived,
where the alcohol factories were,

the sound from them was always there,

and the door to the stairway open
with strange men in it;

and clouds at night
yellow with streetlight.

Rain ran down the cobblestones
to the bottom of the hill

where the smoke-stacks grew,

and women were espaliered on walls,
torn dresses scattered:

the children went home at dawn
to fall from windows.

Near where I lived,
wildflowers bloomed between the stones,

long grass threaded whitely
up to the lintels—

there was broken glass, milk cartons,
a dead kitten.

We gave our toys away before they vanished.

Bronze statues with eyes that looked through you,
bone enameled under the skin,
rain-washed in the open—

the industry went on all the time,
sending up clouds of steam—

a hundred faces giving last looks.

## Christmas in Prague, 1986

The grey smoke of the trees behind the slow snowfall,
the grey walls of the city, like empty bank vaults;

such delicate things are spirits, yet they flicker behind the
snow, the curtain of trees, over the closed

doors and windows; they touch the changeless faces of the
people.
In the gold-makers' land, a man sets up a stall.

In his art, Christ and the Virgin sleep,
three shepherds kneel in adoration—red, yellow, blue—

against the pale horizon. They have no money, but they
look and remember.

The crowds press near, their pockets are empty:
see how they take the snow in their hands to warm it.

An old man steps from the curtain of trees—
his red cloak, his wild hair, blow in the wind.

Soon he is running, his song spills over the snow,
it changes to gold.

What music is this that sets the thousand bells
of the city ringing? What gold coins are these

that chime on the ice in his footsteps?
The people stand, frozen, as the fingers of spirits

press at their throats; as the wild birds of spring

beat their wings in the splintered air;
as their faces blur with weeping.

## Native Land

Three or four farms left now, plus a dog and Mme Hélène,
where on Christmas Eve, 1944, thirty-two young men

were shot by the Germans;

and the forest where one man ran, crossing the road,
jumping a stream.

Fog freezes to the branches—
the dead appear

like sea anemones behind shop windows.

Their village has fallen,
their guards are weeping. White-faced as metal

they exhibit belongings: pocket-watches, a helmet,
self-portraits.

Even the stones are clock-marked with bullets.

Love, we stand in a grove of birches, we pull our coats tight
against the wind. Bullets fly backwards

into the mouths of our guns.

This is the picture to step in:
now we are part of the land.

## My Dear Friends

In the hotel room, a piece of paper has shifted;
there is the smell of sweat. Those were not our hands
opening drawers. Nor are these our soldiers,
dressed in black, searching beneath the train.

A man on hands and knees examines the corridors,
an old woman on a tram takes your arm.
How to explain this?—she wants you to stay;

you must not leave them in this lost city.

My dear friends, someone kneels on the tracks
ahead of you—still will you go?

This city, with its black towers,
its streets where our bodies, like pale
splintered wood, drift—

look at the hillside: in the sun's gold *there*
you see our blood.

These bent heads, these shoes fragile as paper,
the fresh snow, the terrible angels in churches:

we will wait for you. We have come to watch you go.

For the last time we touch hands. Slowly the train
leaves the empty station. When we look back,

it is you who have turned to stone.

Let us drink to the children conceived this summer,
let us touch hands once more.

Let us show you the city that never fell,
the empty city,
where people kneel on the land
and dig under the ashes.

Please, let us show you.

We do not feel the cold.
Our children walk naked on ice.
They lie hidden beneath the trains.

When the soldiers come,
it means nothing.

Prague-Köln-Berlin

*Madrigal,*
*a Lullaby for Xan*


She sleeps, her dreams as clear as diamond edge
that cuts the icy sky in black and white,
the stars are palest candles to her light.

The dark spills over sill and window ledge,
a river foaming bleakly through the night.
She sleeps, her dreams as clear as diamond edge
that cuts the icy sky in black and white.

The wren that sings its heart-song through the sedge,
and braves the hunter hawk in its full flight,
dreams of its mate and nest soon in its sight:
she sleeps, her dreams as clear as diamond edge
that cuts the icy sky in black and white,
the stars are palest candles to her light.

## Letter From Portugal

*Like beautiful bodies of the dead who had not grown old*
*and they shut them, with tears, in a magnificent mausoleum,*
*with roses at the head and jasmine at the feet—*
*this is how desires look that have passed....*

*(from "Desires" by Cavafy)*

I always begin my letters to you with a kiss,
and so you probably think I frequently dream.
Our room has dark turquoise walls
like the sea far below the white chalk cliffs.
The children are sleeping in the alcove,
short, difficult breaths they hold;
I can hear the restaurant down below,
I can hear the knives.
I am speaking to you about my dream of cold,
like beautiful bodies of the dead who had not grown old.

I found a folded map beneath the bed,
I am speaking about the dream of you I had,
and a ship's name printed in gold.
I am reminding you of how our hands touched,
and that it was as though we'd planned it—
blowing out the candle of our love without a reason,
as we parted from each other in a flurry of desperate
leavetakings;
the chance for happiness was not worth risking:
lovers and desires, they only last a season:
they shut them, with tears, in a magnificent mausoleum.

What do you think? It doesn't matter much,
for we live, after all in our hearts.
I shall leave you with a list,
small, perfect as an orchid's eye, as precious:
there are white dog roses on the cliffs,
and geraniums like flames blooming in the heat,
and much to learn from the tide's turning—
navigation by the stars, map-making,
astrolabe and sextant, the use of charts, all neat,
with roses at the head and jasmine at the feet.

Is it the death of love, everywhere, that I'm seeing?
There's a warm breeze, the blown sand stings my skin alive to feeling,
I am at the end of the world (a place called Sagres),
we look across to Cabo Saint Vincent through a haze of flowers,
orange tiled roofs, white-washed walls, the wind rising.
Navigators leave, with visions glorious and vast—
they are blinded by the sun, they lose their reason—
decaying anchors sleep on the shore, the leavers' leavings—
I see everything as if in a photograph with double cast:
this is how desires look that have passed.

## Tranquille

I return to the bees,
to the cloud of them that razored the air
above the path to Roxana's house,

their white hives in two rows
like a landing field below—

they were swaying, like a giant bell
on an invisible dancer,

or as if the Mediterranean sea curled
and lipped at them.

Your bees, King Gargoris, colonizing
to the furthest reaches of the west,

the cold Pacific.

I had left you by then.
The liquidizing melt

of skin on skin,

the slow casting glances
from sky to river as we turned

were adrift like messages
in bottles. I could not track them,

had no idea where or when
they would turn up.

Until this,
the great bee kingdom.

I ached to dance the ringing bee dance,
strip clean

and clasp the cutting bees around my wrists
for bracelets.

I ached for honey, pain, and you.

The bees, in swarm, moved off.
Roxana, trailing golden nets,
came to gather them.

She, like some priestess
of that far off time

was veiled, slow and sure

as the sky, the sea,
the moon, the unharmed world.

I felt the golden kernel
kick to life inside.

I turned to run,
could smell the pines,

the heat, the blood that ran
when I refused to yield to you,

and sensed, again, the growing
child within the knives:

the myths are all of him,
I do not figure.

Roxana, carrying bees, murmurs,
*Tranquille. Tranquille.*

*Flowers*


What are these flowers
that I pull from my fingers,
their roots in my veins,

their colour and fluid
my breath and bone?

Sweet flowers that need no tending.
My arms ache with the weight of them,

the violet and pansy,
which sprang from the blood of Attis
as he maimed himself, and smelled the sweet scent
of the pine.

But there is no blood here.

I spread my hands like fans on the pale sheets
and behold the flowers while you are quiet, sleeping.

I touch your cheek. My fingers leave a print.

You turn, stirring the flowers, the pines,
the white bedcover, the sea I was born in.

*Antiquities,*

we lie on the soft bank of the river,
flies walk the sharp trajectories

of shoulder blades
and hips,

in the centre of the pelvic bones
are discs—

two golden suns engraved with antelope.
The surprise is steel,

the tip of a spade
that chinks,

and the hand within a glove
that tries my rings.

I was blind,
I felt the history of your tongue

for one last time on my eyes:
I would have spoken,

I would have cried our love aloud,
but they broke us

like pottery or glass,
anything else that doesn't last.

THE MERCERS

## The House at Mercer's Cove

Tomorrow is Sunday.
I go to the kitchen to peel the vegetables.

I gather up my sewing.

In the morning we have breakfast—salt fish
from the storehouse.

At lunch we wash the dishes.

We read the Bible, sing some hymns,
have supper,

then lay the large white cloth
over the table.

Unnecessary work can wait till Monday.

I forgot to say that the house has small framed windows.
It is made of wood, and freshly painted for winter.

Where could I go? To Lizzie's?
Aunt Prudence up the hill?

The girls from here work as maids in Montreal.

## In the Front Room

is an organ.
I look past it to the ocean.

My sister's husband's son
disappeared from a boat,

my sister's husband's sister
went away down south:

she never came back,
dead, we think,

in a train wreck.

Three bedrooms, a dining room and living room,
the back kitchen:

I can drive the sleigh when I want
to Coley's Point.

Partridge berries after the first hard frost,
hot bakeapple drink for the children,

you'd give the mummers a bit of cake and a glass of clingy
when they'd come.

No drinking.
No dancing (except, perhaps, for the R.C.'s).
No playing cards.

Lamb cooked for dinner on Good Friday,
and herring.

I comb my hair.
I put on a dress and collar.

I dance in my room.
I try on rings.

My fingers make no sound.

I look past the cliff to Coley's Point
where the birds whirl round.

I see the split in the sky
where the angels fly.

I see the break in the sea
where the boats dance, helplessly.

I take off my rings.
I look out at the sky, the sea, the road,
the truth.

## *When the Men are Gone to Sea*


we do the garden.  We cut the hay, spread it to dry,
and rake it into a pook.

We have the garden, and the hens and the haying.

I sit at night by the open door and tear up rags.
Blue for my eyes (and his!),
brown for my hair,
red, yellow, green, orange,
the colours of the hills.

You never see a man up here in summer:
they're all gone down to Labrador.

If you see one you wonder,
knit stockings for winter

(blue,
brown).

## I Lie Down

on the ice on the bay.
The stars swim slowly by.

This is the pain the men feel when they drown,
this is why they won't swim.

Men and women, a linked chain
crossing the ocean from Jersey Island.

This is all I know of my family.

The ice shapes itself to my body.
I feel tongues of ice on my bones.

I make a list of the vegetables
we put in the cellar:
cabbage, carrots, onions, beets and turnips.

We've a pig to kill for Christmas.

I've made a doll with blueberries for eyes,
for Zelah.

Black currant, gooseberries, wild raspberries
on low bushes.

Still the cold plays its scales of music.

Apple trees.  Cherry trees.
These are like dreams,

heat-soaked,
sweet, saltless.

I lick the tears that freeze at my nostrils.

My father would laugh if he saw me like this,
then whip me.

## I Touched the Swelling

on the child's wrist
and felt the knob of pain.

I held that flower
and gently breathed away its petals.

I could put my hand on a red-hot stove and not be burned.
I could wake up hungry
and find bread in the fields.

A storm blows in.

I pull down the blinds, and throw the kitchen mats
across the stove to spare us lightning.

Here is what we owed once Gosse took most of the fish
at the end of the season:

money to pay the doctor, the church, the school.

## The Black Horse

is gone.
I've walked the fifteen miles to get her
more than once.

I sent Dorcas to borrow some books from Prudence.
"Tell your sister she's read all the books we've got.
Tell her to read her Bible," she said.

The R.C.'s draw their blinds.
King Billy's flags fly over the road.

Rock, meadow, the sea,
this is my world.

The men belong to the Orange Lodge.

## One Heater to Heat the Whole House

Once you went to bed in those feather mattresses,
you couldn't move.

Everyone had gardens.
Now they've all gone to the commons.

Father's Bible in four volumes....

My love. So much to do before bad weather sets in.

And you gone long before, stepping off along the shoreline,
land for your children.

EIGHT POEMS FOR MARGARET
July-August, 1989

The packers are done.
The three-quarter moon slips through the sky
in slow time.

You lie in the bath.
Your tennis shorts—a gift to me—
blow on the line.

The house is quiet,
all the things you loved in it, gone.

The garden was all your care:
nasturtium, rose, chrysanthemum,
cat mint—

the two black cats
from next door,
roll in it—

black-eyed susan, and sweet pea,
gentians, alyssum;

the bird house filled with bread;

roses that colour the spaces between
the spin-around clothes line

where your tennis shorts swing.

Pink clouds colour the city
where Margaret once ran,

her steps bright as water in sunshine.

Now you lift a thin thigh from the bath—
tomorrow we're going.

You had prizes at school for needlepoint and
singing...

the open mouths of the livingston daisies,
closing.

♥

She dreams of falling,
but it is not she who slips
through the rails,

it is the white figure of a girl,
or the ghost of a girl
who has never lived.

Margaret is too substantial to fall
or to be pushed:
it is unimaginable.

I put on her old tennis shorts,
fresh from the line,

and go out in the garden.
Dry soil breaks in my hands.

She said here, plant the roses here,
they will not fail.

♥

A white butterfly
flips past the window,

over the stair-rail
and down, I presume,

into the garden.
What a garden it is!

Twenty wasp stings for the poor man
building our fence—

we have found him a bee-hat since—

wood left over from building,
and pink tufts of insulation

flapping, like sea-wrack.

Underneath it all, Margaret,
as you can see,

are the ferns and moss,
and bluish-white Indian pipe

so ghostly a hue;

and the gooseberries—
the canes almost hidden, bent by the weight
of the fruit:

they lie on the earth
and are heaped with pine-needles,

trash, leaves, dog feces, compost.
We have plans for this place:

with you I've mapped a rose-garden
where the warped and windy shed stands.

The cats will forgive us tearing it down,
though they haunt it now

as if there were no other refuge.

*Refuge*, why that word now,
when I am helpless to help you?

♥

The moon rose upside down
in Africa, you say.

A good day. The drugs mute the pain,

you forget why.

You iron a few shirts, grow tired,
watch golf on television,

have tea with friends.
The day, for me, drones on.

I fix photographs into an album,
finish the ironing.

Ask God again how could he be so
wrong.

There is thunder this evening,
the dog cowers in the kitchen.

I lean on the stove, uselessly weeping.

♥

My bed is my island,
my refuge.

But what is a bed to you
in the night hours

that toll
to the treble of your radio?

Even in my grief
I can turn across the swell

and find love,
mute now in its terror for you,

but there, afloat.

What comforts you?
Just the radio.

You lie in a hospital bed at home.
You will not let me raise it up
to ease you.

It is only a bed, your stubbornness tells me.

You wrap your hair in curlers.
I do not know what gives you the strength
to do it.

Oh plain death. You have no mirror.

I turn in bed to touch my husband's hand.

Not in my house,
she won't die here, we won't let her,
he says.

We hear thunder,
and brace ourselves.

♥

I sit up in bed and say it aloud—
*Hope.*

In the morning we consult the bird book,
arguing over robins *here* and *there*.
Ours are bigger, a kind of thrush.
Margaret's are small, bright feathered,
birds she's known all her life.

Who's right?

I mop and dust and vacuum.
The baby cleans and polishes all the stones.

Good-morning. I am a spirit in search of
wind, snow, sun.
I am a soul marooned in ice;
I am swimming the band of water
that swims the earth,
the universe,

the chorus of spirits.

I am holding my breath and travelling through this unknown
sea without a mask.

♥

The wind shakes the trees,
salty and sweet.

Margaret sits in a deck chair,
sleeping.

Say a word to her and she is, at once,
awake.

But she is tapping her way, eyes closed,
into another landscape.

The new fence is almost finished,
the dogs roam its edges

and pee on it.
What is the word for 'escape'?

Margaret knows it.

She sits up to ask if a debt has been paid,
to say she is too much trouble,

to speak of her son's young friend,
years ago.

"He's in jail now," she says sadly.
She cannot get up.

Yesterday we lost the key to the medicine box.
Had the baby hidden it,

or was this a way to tell us, 'enough is enough'?
What line is being crossed

as she shifts her thin legs
on the chair slats?

She says she smells roses—
fine gardener that she is,

the labour and pleasure of those years
follow her.

We sort herbs into jars:
they are musky and tepid in odour.

Roses, she says, roses. The sweetness
makes her smile. The scent that pursued the saints

billows about her.

♥

Now is the time
for rejoicing at her life,

at the wind that quarters the trees,
and the sun and cool morning.

As when the 1st battalion
of the West African Frontier Regiment

played, for her, the Hausa Farewell
as she left Nigeria,

so now there is a salute to be given.

Let the wind give it,
and the trees,

and the light beyond this room.

Let her be stepping now,
as she walked, in 1948,

up the airplane steps,
boldly under the sun,

while the band played.

*Blow far winds blow,
the east cold.*

*Margaret has gathered her gifts
about her,*

*she walks the white stones.*

♥

A COLD DEPARTURE:
*The Liaison of George Sand and Fryderyk Chopin*

♥ George Sand's Letter
*George Sand to Wojciech Grzymala in Paris*
*Nohant, June 1838*

*It would never occur to me to doubt your sincerity.*
*Let us state the question clearly:*
*one must put one's own happiness last*
*when the happiness of those we love*
*claims all our strength.*

I looked at the sun—
a yellow pinhole
with blackness all around it.

I looked at the skeleton
inside my hands:

the fingers danced
like black burnt sticks.
I looked at my heart:
it curled at the edges,

its juice spilled
into the cavity
of my body.

I put my hands in there:
the little black sticks stirred—

there was nothing there
for you.

I moved my knees,
I lifted my feet
and danced in the colour yellow.

I made claw-marks in the earth:
I scratched its lens.

I made a wound
and watered it from the heart.
I carried it in my hands

and brought it to you.

Is this what is meant by love,
by happiness?

♥

Give me a clear, straightforward and categorical answer.
Is she the right one to secure his happiness?
I am not asking whether he loves her.
What I want to know is which of the two of us he must
give up. His nature seems too unstable
to stand great anguish.

I will not battle with his childhood friend.
We did not deceive each other. All the same,
we had to come back to earth
when the divine flame had cooled.
The song of angels beckons us heavenwards.
For myself I refuse to give way to passion.
Heaven is where we meet. So my duty is fully mapped.

But I can, without forswearing myself,
perform it two distinct ways.
I could slip into his thoughts.
I could from time to time permit a chaste embrace.
I could keep as far as possible away {from Chopin}.

The man is on the bed.
I lie next to him.
This boat steers itself.
I think we will drown.

Sea-beasts rise from the floor:
I cannot remember more.
I promise you

they were not of this world.

Which of the two of us,
who surrenders?

It is an easy birth,

but I have no recollection
of having done it.

The man on the bed—
as I rolled away from his body,
as I drew a circle of prayer—

there was a waterfall of colour.

So I shut my eyes
and swam.

♥

*Marriage or any similar union would be the graveyard*
*of his artist soul. Happiness*
*as a family man is out of the question.*
*It will be for you to tell me if I am wrong.*

*I am convinced one is a better human being*
*when one loves with sublime emotion.*
*One rather draws near to God.*

*I have no wish to steal anyone from anyone—*
*I have too much respect for the notion of property—*
*unless it be prisoners from their gaolers,*
*victims from their executioners,*
*Poland from Russia.*

*Nothing is so precious as a fatherland,*
*and a man who has one already must not make unto himself*
*a new one.*

And the Lord said unto me, Give,
and I held out my hand.

And the Lord said unto me, Give,
and I held out my other hand.

And he said again, Give.
I looked at the trees that were bending.
I said, Lord, I would do anything.

He said, Give.

I said, Lord I have had visions and dreams.

He said, Give.

I began to weep. He said, Give.
I began to sing:

and dreamt that I swam naked at midnight,
and dreamt that I swam away from my husband,
and dreamt that I hid from my children under a stone.

A white stone. Then a black stone.
I dreamt that the Lord kept moving the stones.

And the Lord said, Give.

Consumed am I by thy fire.
By the fire of the pit.
The cypress trees are wilted, scorched, burnt up.

The Lord said, Give.

White foamy milk poured from my breasts.
My child cried and cried.

I would do anything, Lord, I said.

Everyone is born like a stone slipping
down inside a dress.
A smooth stone

that falls quickly.

A mother bends and picks it up.
She warms it in her hand.

Years later, turning out the pockets
of an old coat, she finds it.

Tears come to her eyes.

Everyone who is born is in pain.
Everyone is fearful of strangers.

He said, Give.

Here is my body, Lord.
It melts like wax. It is a candle in the earth.

He said, Give, give, give.

♥

*I shall represent for him an Italy*
*which one visits and enjoys on spring days*
*but where one cannot remain permanently,*
*because there is more sunshine than beds and tables.*

*Poor Italy! A land that one dreams of,*
*longs for or regrets;*
*but where no one can remain, since she herself is unhappy*
*and cannot impart a happiness she does not possess.*

On a train travelling
through the mountains of Italy:
lake after lake, white-cliffed,
fathomless,
inviting.

A villa on a hillside,
a trip down into town:

at Como the lake
licks the city walls.

We play house in the villa:
floors and tables,
cutting boards,

a gecko in a marble drawer
with dusty cutlery.

At night bonfires prick the shore.

One white sheet on the balcony.
Brought in.

♥

There is one last supposition that it is right
for me to mention. It may be that he no longer loves
this childhood friend at all.
My good friend, be his guardian angel.
You must save him from the too relentless claims
of conscience, save him from his own virtue.

Whoever, in return for a certain
finite amount of devotion, calls for the devotion
of another's whole future life
is asking something wicked.

I loathe seducers. A vow of love and faithfulness
is crime and cowardice when the lips utter
what the heart disavows.

We shall not see each other every day;
every day we shall not be consumed by the sacred fire,
but there will be some fine days and some holy flames.

The dance you dance
is east to west:

each step of the dance
is a wish.

The dance you dance now
is the dance of naming women.

I give up my name.
I give up my dancing feet.
I give up my spirit.

A green meadow on the sea,
a house with seven rooms to think in:

keep him safe,
keep him with me.

I sit and overcome my pain.

My heart is an agony. For you are there
and I touch you here,

here.

♥

*I have sometimes been mistaken about people*
*but never about myself. My feelings have always*
*been stronger than my rational thinking,*
*and the boundaries I have tried to fix for myself*
*have proved useless.*

*I have changed my ideas a score of times.*
*Above all I have believed in faithfulness.*
*Others have failed me and I have failed them;*
*yet I felt no remorse.*

*Whenever I was unfaithful I was the victim*
*of a kind of fatality,*
*of my own instinctive urge towards the ideal,*
*which compelled me to leave what was imperfect*
*for something which seemed closer to perfection.*

What did we think we could do for each other?
Enter a mirror?

What looks back through the glass
is a spirit trying to enter itself.

Everything inside the mirror is dead.

This is my gift:
I stepped inside.

♥

*I have loved as an artist, as a woman, a sister, a mother,*
*a nun, a poet. Some of these loves have been born*
*and have died in a single day.*
*Some have driven me to despair,*
*others have kept me cloistered in a state*
*of extreme spirituality.*

*And all the time I have been perfectly sincere.*

*My whole nature moved into these different phases.*
*I have appeared what I truly am:*
*one who revels in all that is beautiful,*
*who is hungry for the truth, sensitive in her feelings,*
*weak in her judgments, often ridiculous, always sincere,*
*never petty or vindictive,*
*not inclined to suffer fools gladly and, thank God,*
*quick to forget evil things and evil people.*

I stood at the door of the clinic.
I carried my baby in my arms.

I put a stone on the table.
I said, Here, doctor, eat my bread.

I put white stars on the table.
I said, Here, doctor, eat my fire.

I put the torn fabric of the sky
on the table.
I said, Here, doctor, cover the dead
with this.

I put the baby on the table.
I dressed her in stones and fire.
I dressed her in rags.
I married her to the dead.

I said, Here, doctor, set me on fire.
I put a match on the table.

I said, Here, doctor, build me a house.
I put smoke on the table.

I said, Here, doctor, cut me with this.
I put my hands on the table.

I lifted up my child.
She had bread, a wedding dress,
she had a house roofed with blood.

I said, Here, doctor, take my life.
I said, Here, doctor, breathe the baby alive.

He said, No.
I am too tired.
He said, No.

I put my knife on the table.
I opened my mouth.
The table drowned in blood.

He said, No.

♥

*There my dear friend, you have my life.*
*You see it is nothing to boast of.*
*There is nothing to admire, much to be pitied,*
*nothing which a kind heart will condemn.*

*I am certain that those who accuse me*
*of having been an evil woman have lied,*
*and I could easily prove it if I took the trouble*
*to draw on my memories and tell my story:*

*but I have not the patience to do it,*
*and my memories are as short-lived as my rancours.*

I can taste the baby.
The shock of her pain.

I can taste her blindness.

I can taste the baby—
her life runs away
like liquid,

her life dances like infant birds
aroused by a scream.

Her life curls and uncurls
against my dead thighs.

I can taste the baby
at the moment you leave me.

You have my life:
put it in human shape.

You have my life:
find it.

You have my life:
I hear it crying, abandoned
in a Spanish *caverna*.

My mouth touches your mouth,
and I taste the lives of infants.

This is my baby, my baby.

I lose her.

♥

*I have never deceived anyone*
*and have never ceased to be faithful*
*unless I had very strong reasons which*
*through another's fault, had killed my love.*

*I am not of an inconstant nature. On the contrary,*
*I am so used to giving my exclusive affection*
*to one who loves me truly, so slow to take fire,*
*so accustomed to living with men without reflecting*
*that I am a woman,*

*that I was rather disturbed and frightened at the effect*
*this little person {Chopin} had on me.*

*I still have not got over my amazement.*
*It was a case of sudden invasion*
*and it is not in my nature to regulate my conduct*
*by reason when love takes command.*

*So I am not blaming myself;*
*but I can plainly see that I am still very susceptible*
*and frailer than I thought I was.*

Sleep descends on me
like a dove.

Its metal cry
is in my ears.

I swallow it whole,
where it is imprisoned.

Living creatures, letters,
music,

the children you cannot have—
I open myself to these,

and we dance, we two,
me and you.

Your thought is my thought.
In this secret place

we dance with elegance.
All the tortures are ours,
and the pleasures.

A tree clicks its dry leaves.

I look up at the apples,
I close my eyes

while light falls through the open window
of the sky above.

They want us to go on
although we have given up:

the gods who don't exist,
who refuse to accept us.

♥

What does it matter? It saddens me.
I shall have to tell lies like the rest of them.
That, I can assure you, is more mortifying
to my good opinion of myself
than to be mocked for a bad novel
or hissed for a bad play.

I should have kept a better watch over my eyes
and ears and, above all my heart.

But if Heaven would have us remain faithful
to earthly affections, why does it sometimes
allow angels to lose their way among us
and meet us in our paths?

—

I love you,
but still you doubt.

We are changed in the light of that fact.
Touch.

Your hand splits the shadow
from the lamp.

You open the window.

I am the shadow.
You are the dance.

♥


You are gone.
The cup of tea cools;
leaves stir in the corner

beneath the open window:

*And so the great question of love
arises once more within me.*

What shall I do with it?

I turn it over.
I prick it with a needle:

it leaks a clear liquid.
It could be tears.

♥

*When one has allowed one's soul to be invaded,*
*when one has granted the simplest caress,*
*urged to it by the feeling of love,*
*the infidelity has already been committed.*

*What follows is less serious,*
*for he who has lost the heart has lost everything.*

*Hence, as a matter of principle,*
*I think that a total consecration of the new bond*
*does little to aggravate the initial fault,*
*but rather that the attachment may become more human*
*more powerful and dominating after possession.*

*That is quite probable, and even certain.*

*And so, when two persons wish to live together,*
*they should not violate nature and truth*
*by retreating from a complete union.*
*If he had asked for it in Paris*
*I should have yielded.*

All winter I have watched the light fade,

all spring I have waited for your hand
to lift me above the round world

like the moon,

like the womb that dreamed me,

like the spin
of a foreign sea.

You love my daughter.
We love you.

You love your mother.
I will write to her.

You love my son—
take everything you want—

my memories will begin
with you.

I hear my father.
The horse stops at the scene
of his accident—

I get off
and listen for death.

The trees are my music.

I have no tongue,
it is here, on paper.

I have no body,
it is counting money.

Soon someone must come
to save us.

♥

*It will cost me dear to see our angel {Chopin} suffer.*
*I am not a child. I could well observe*
*that his human passion was making rapid strides*
*and that it was time we kept apart.*
*That is why, the night before I left, I did not wish*
*to be left alone with him and I practically turned you both*
*out of doors.*

*And since I am telling you everything,*
*I wish to say that he displeased me by one single thing—*
*the fact that he had had in his own mind the wrong reason*
*for abstaining.*
*Until that moment I had considered it a fine thing*
*that he abstained out of respect for me, out of shyness,*
*even out of fidelity to another.*
*It was that which charmed and allured me the most in him.*
*But just as he was leaving, as if to overcome a final*
*temptation, he said two or three words*
*which did not at all correspond to my ideas.*

*He seemed to despise the coarser side of human nature,*
*and to fear to soil our love by further ecstasy.*
*I have always loathed this way of looking*
*at the final embrace of love.*

These stones that we lay on the path,
the white shells that spell
your name,

the violets
dusted with sand—

these are permanent.

Not the wickedness,
not the evil thought

that entered your brain,
not the dish that shattered.

I wanted to kill you—
but is that our love?

We cut an orange,
we share;

there are guests, invited
and uninvited:

is that our love?

There was a horse on a road,
there was the corpse of my father:

was that our love?

Touch these stones,
these shells,

brush the sand from the petals.

Whatever sadness you have
is not our love.

Take the whole orange
and eat it.

♥

*Can there be for lofty natures a purely physical love,*
*and for sincere natures a love which is purely intellectual?*
*Can there ever be love without a single kiss,*
*and a kiss of love without sensual pleasure?*
*Tell me, what wretched woman has left him with such*
*impressions of physical love.*

*Poor angel. They should hang all women who make vile*
*in men's eyes that which in all creation is most holy*
*and most worthy of respect, the divine mystery,*
*the sublimest and most serious act of universal life.*
*The magnet draws the iron to it....*
*This is a frightful letter.*
*It is my ultimatum.*

I said to the man:
there is a black bag,

I am afraid of what you have in it.

I said to the man:
you have a black bag,

I am afraid of what you have in it.

I am finished.
I am made of stone.

You cannot open me up.
Put your knives away in your sack.

I said to the man,
I am finished,
put the stones back
and sew me up.

I said to the baby,
I shall sew you into the sack.

I sewed her up.

Her head broke the stitches.
Her arms and legs broke the stitches.
She ran away.

I said to the man who knocked at the door,
here is a knife.

I said to the angel,
here is a rope.

Cut the baby out,
hang the woman.
I am sick to death
of feeding them.

I said to the angel,
I will feed you.

I said to the man,
I will feed you.

I put the stones in a circle.
I lit the fire.

I stirred the pot of stones
and waited.

♥

*If his happiness depends, or is going to depend,*
*on her,*
*let him go his way.*
*If he is to be unhappy, prevent it.*
*I am ready to sacrifice myself for one I love.*


Something is absent.

I check my desk
for books and drawings,

I touch the children's beds
next door;

the closet—my hat, cape, boots,
all are there.

I pick up my walking stick:

the night-table, the music stand,
the piano,

the window, lawn, roadway, stars,

the Mediterranean sea,

the church we did not attend,
the marriage we did not have—

all these are present.

What is it?

I tap my stick.
It becomes a clock.
How long has it been since we met?

I take the horse
and ride to Paris.

I visit all our friends.
There are men, women,
engagements, performances.

There is a boat in a dream.

It travels down a river.
It goes on forever.

What has happened to the Revolution,
to Liberty?

This is not a riddle:

enough blood was spilled
to require an answer.

♥

*You must tell me the plain truth.*
*Don't say a word to the boy {Chopin}.*
*I see only intimate friends, darlings like you,*
*who have never thought evil of those whom they love.*

*We shall have comfortable talks*
*and your depressed spirit will revive in the country air.*
*If the boy doesn't want to come, leave him alone;*

*he is afraid of what people might say,*
*he is afraid of I know not what.*

This passion is a country
without any future:

food untasted,
words mistranslated.

The country expands,
acquires new territory:

day-time and night-time
it records a history.

I examine the atlas,
I put a pin in the map

and send out soldiers.
Some ecstasy,
some tiresome quarrels:

if I knew what to hope for
I should have no more worries,

make jam in the country,
look elsewhere.

♥

*In creatures I love*
*I respect everything I do not understand.*
*Search in the depths of his soul—*
*I must know what is going on there.*

*You know me by heart now.*
*I send you my warmest regards, dear kind friend.*

*I felt I was speaking to my other self,*
*the best and dearest of the two.*

I come back to the emptiness
inside me,

to the cavity where the baby was,
to the inexhaustible wish to have.

I am extravagant,
yet I live on nothing.

I light one candle.

Now the armies are at the door,

their barges on the river,
their horses covered in blood.

My father died long ago
by a roadside.

I go to the hospital—
the nearby houses are empty—

a soldier offers his pillow.

I touch the bandage,
I help him sit,
I lift his legs up.

He is cold,
his skin prickles.

I lie down with him in my arms.

Tell me what to do,
how to defend him {Chopin}.

♥

♥ Chopin's Letters

## Love As It Is

I have spoken to the dead.
I have broken my word.
But the dead are all I have.

They ask questions:
where are we?
Are we crossing a bridge?

They are like children.

I look at a tree.
Birds range its branches,
colours slip from lime to silver,

and the dead say, "What is it?"

The bridge moves,
slipping on plates, edging, easing;

the earth turns, and the moon and stars:
they twist free of the hand that spins them.

The dead say, "Are we at rest?"
Yes, and yes.

♥

*I have seen her three more times. It seems*
*like only a day. She gazed deep into my eyes*
*while I played...such dark strange eyes she had.*
*What were they saying? She leaned against the piano*
*and her eyes seemed to caress mine. I was overcome.*
*My soul seemed to find its haven in the smile of those*
*remarkable eyes. I longed for them...my heart*
*was conquered...I have seen her twice since...*
*one time alone. She loves me!*
*Aurore! What a charming name! Like the dawn*
*it banishes darkness.*

*July 1838, Paris*


Now I will tell you about the voices.
I do not hear them, I speak them.

I speak before I hear.
I do not know what I say, but I am healed
by speaking.

I speak the tongues I reached for.
Through great effort I reached for joy.

Now I do not know what I have,
unless it is praise,
yes, perhaps truly, that is it:

for the exaltation of all gifts,
for the trees especially, and the broad
river of the spirit.

The child looks at the sea and asks if that
is the angel.

It is restless enough.
We look and look at the sea.

We throw stones,
and hold our breath.

♥

I hear the horses shifting their weight
in the field.

I hear the strands of grass rub
the damp earth.

The horses stand as if they belonged,
and could slip across the frost or sun
into forest—

yet they stay.

Their breath is like clouds
of stirring mosquitoes; their heat

flames through the glass.
I put my hand over my eyes and turn back
to my paper.

I write music.

We stand in the field next to the horses.
My joints remember bruises,
the stretch of mounting.

My wrists click as I lift your child.
We stand like drawings.

♥

*or rather Valldemosa, a few miles away; between the cliffs
and the sea a huge deserted Carthusian monastery where
in a cell with doors larger than any carriage-gateway
in Paris you may imagine me with my hair unkempt,
without white gloves and pale as ever. The cell is shaped
like a tall coffin, the enormous vaulting covered with dust,
the window small. In front of the window are orange-trees,
palms, cypresses; opposite the window is my camp-bed under a
Moorish filigree rose-window. Close to the bed is an old
square grubby box which I can scarcely use for writing on,
with a leaden candlestick (a great luxury here) and a little
candle. Bach, my scrawls and someone else's old
papers...silence...you can yell... still silence.*

*To Julian Fontana in Paris*

I call my mother who made me.
I call my father who made me.
I call the birch trees,
the wind, the snow.
I call the rivers of blood of the moon,
I call the silvery mineral earth,
I call the circle of my childhood,
the horses.

Bind me with their binding.
Bind me with their healing.
Bind me with the circle of love
that is their healing.
I bless the wind for strength.
I bless the snow for music.
I bless the red moon for its dancing movement.
I bless the vegetable earth for its final resting.
I bless the wheel of horses,
I bless the face of a child at a window,
I bless the entry into the circle.

Heal my spirit.

♥

*They tell me that I am better...But I feel that*
*deep down in myself, something is wrong.*
*Aurore's eyes are misted: they shine only when*
*I play, and only then is the world full of*
*light and beauty...I fear she knows something*
*about my condition she cruelly keeps from me in*
*the mistaken belief she is sparing me new pain.*

*June 1839*

I put my hands in the earth,
I put the earth in my mouth.

I put the sea in my mouth.
I put colour in my mouth.

I light the candle.
A moth swings on the pendulum
of its life.
I trap it and free it.
It comes back.

Knock, knock, goes the wind.
The cypresses scrape the sand.
I read the handwriting:

I run the tap of my blood.

The world is my shadow,
I embrace the light.

*Tonight the moon is marvelous.*
*Never have I seen it like this. But, but!*

Please empty my soul of this fear,
please empty my soul of the beating of drums,
please empty my soul of debt,
please empty my soul of disappointment.

Water of the night, the stilling rain,
water of the day, on the tongue,
water of the hour,
water of belief:

I embrace you.

*I am living in my cell and sometimes have Arabian dances*
*and African sunshine. Then there is the Mediterranean. I'm*
*not sure, but I think I shan't come back before May or even*
*later. Hand over my letter and the Preludes to Pleyel*
*yourself.*

*Write.*

*To Julian Fontana in Paris*
*Valldemosa, 22 January 1839*

♥

*I feel strange here this year: in the morning I often look into the room next to mine, but there is no one there...I keep going into your room and into the one next door where the Mistress is working—but at this moment I am far away— as usual in some strange region of space. Of course they are only those imaginary spaces—but I am not ashamed...I have written three new Mazurkas....*

*To his Family in Warsaw*
*Nohant, 16-20 July 1845*

My ancestors inhabit my bones.
My bones are like numbers.
My fingers make designs,
I can hear them.

I place my hand on my chest,
I cross the other one over it.
I get no sleep at all.

My heart aches to be opened.
My spirit reaches, and falls back.

Is it tears that I make into music?
You can hear them break, like glass.
I collect them in a vial,
and spill them on paper.

♥

*It is thundery today and rather hot.*
*The gardener is transplanting flowers.*
*The giraffe, which I believe Louise and Kalasanty saw, has*
*died. I wish I never had any sadder news than that to report*
*to you.*

*I play a little and write a little. Sometimes I am satisfied*
*with my 'cello sonata, sometimes not. I throw it aside and*
*then take it up again. I have three new mazurkas.*
*When one is doing something it seems all right, otherwise one*
*would not write anything. It is only later that one reflects*
*carefully, and either keeps a thing or rejects it.*
*Time is the best form of censorship and patience the finest*
*teacher.*

*It is five o'clock and already so dark that I can hardly see.*
*I must stop now. In a month I shall send more news.*

*To his family in Warsaw*
*Finished 19th April, 1847*

Dust. Clouds of it that I cough.
A whirlwind, black as a sheath,
a horse snorting foam flecked with blood.

I imagine the sea,
a sweep of meadow decked with bluebells.
You, well, picnicking with children.

They have faces like dishes.
I paint ears on them
and then I listen;

I paint their mouths,
small red bows that open and close,

tongues like smooth ribbon.

I listen: I hear the rattle of teeth,
the intake of breath,

I hear them sobbing as you walk, knee deep
through the grasses, chest deep in the breakers.

I paint it over.
Blue for eyes, this time.

They turn and aim them like bullets,

I paint sunflowers:

they wave at you, swimming.

Parentheses for nostrils,
a handkerchief.

A black cloud swirls in a funnel.
Its cone touches the plate of the earth

and tilts it.

You slip off, in a fall of water
like music.

♥

*One need not fully record all that has been said and done. Mme Sand can have nothing but good memories of me in her heart, if she ever looks back on the past...it is a fever for which there is no cure in cases where the imagination is so dominant and the victim is let loose on shifting and uncertain ground. Well, they say "even a cypress-tree may have its caprices."*

*To his Family in Warsaw*
*Paris, Christmas 1847*

The air moved over her back.
The air that was not air, that was cold,
moved across her shoulder.

She lay sleeping,
golden.

Inside the door,
the door that opened into a cave,

I stood up.
The cold air moved over my arm and shoulder.

I danced to it.
The air swayed away.

Then it fell.  The door fell
on my chest, and shut.

If I were made of light, or air,
I would dance,
rise to the rim of the sky,

touch the stars,
fall, all of a piece
on the world.

I would never have left her
for less.

♥

*I had thought that a few months spent apart from Chopin would heal the wound, make possible a tranquil friendship, and pour balm on memory. I saw him for a moment in March, 1848. I took his hand. It was as cold as ice, and trembling. I should have liked to talk with him, but he fled. It was my turn to say that he no longer loved me, but I spared him that pain, and left everything in the lap of the gods—and the future. I never saw him again.*

George Sand

## Acknowledgments

I would like to thank *The Canadian Forum, Exile Magazine, Hawthorne Poetry Newsletter, The Malahat Review*, and *Women's Education des Femmes* in which some of these poems have appeared. "George Sand's Letter", which was published in *Exile Magazine*, received the National Magazine Award for Poetry, silver. It was included in *A Cold Departure*, produced by Don Mowat and broadcast on CBC Radio.

I am also grateful to the Canada Council for its support during the writing of some of these poems.

Excerpts from George Sand and Fryderyk Chopin's letters are taken, in the main, from *Selected Correspondence of Fryderyk Chopin* translated and edited by Arthur Hedley, William Heinemann Ltd., Great Britain, 1962.

Note: "Tranquille" pg. 15: King Gargoris is said to have been the discoverer of honey. He appears in legends of the mysterious Tartessian civilization generally thought to have its home in the Guadalquivir basin from around 1500 to 500 B.C. He had a son, Habis, by one of his daughters. Habis was known, partly because he taught his people to plough with oxen, as 'the civilizing' monarch. Nothing more is known about his mother.